This student workbook is intended to reinforce your understanding of the three units of substantive content (scientific explanations and evidence), plus the procedural content (How Science Works), on the new single award GCSE Physics specification from AQA.

The questions in your objective tests / written exams will combine elements from both substantive and procedural content, so to answer them you will have to recall relevant scientific facts and draw upon your knowledge of how science works.

Every worksheet is cross-referenced to the revision guide, *The Essentials of AQA GCSE Physics*, published by Lonsdale.

The questions on pages 4–11 of this workbook will test your understanding of the key concepts covered in How Science Works. In addition, there are individual How Science Works question pages throughout this book, which are designed to make sure you know how to apply your knowledge, for example to evaluate topical social-scientific issue.

 In this workbook, any questions that cover content which will only be tested on Higher Tier test papers appear inside clearly labelled boxes.

## Note to Teachers

The pages in this workbook can be used as…
- classwork sheets – students can use the revision guide to answer the questions
- harder classwork sheets – pupils study the topic and then answer the questions without using the revision guide
- easy-to-mark homework sheets – to test pupils' understanding and reinforce their learning
- the basis for learning homework tasks which are then tested in subsequent lessons
- test material for topics or entire units
- a structured revision programme prior to the objective tests / written exams.

Answers to these worksheets are available to order.

**ISBN: 978-1-905129** _ _ _

Published by Lonsdale, a division of Huveaux Plc

**Project editor**: Charlotte Christensen
**Cover and concept design**: Sarah Duxbury
**Designer**: Graeme Browne

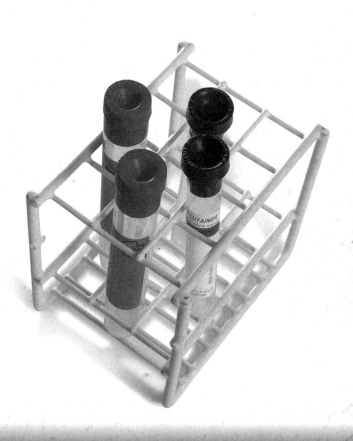

# Contents

# Contents

The numbers in brackets correspond to the reference numbers on the AQA GCSE Physics specification.

# How Science Works

## How Science Works

**The following questions are designed to make sure you understand what the How Science Works element of your AQA GCSE science course is all about.**

**1** Only one statement in each of the following sets is accurate. Read them all carefully and then place a tick beside the correct one.

a) **i** The term 'How Science Works' refers to a set of key concepts. ☐

  **ii)** The term 'How Science Works' refers to a set of unanswered questions. ☐

  **iii)** The term 'How Science Works' refers to a set of scientific facts. ☐

b) **i)** How Science Works is only relevant to physics. ☐

  **ii)** How Science Works is relevant to all areas of science. ☐

  **iii)** How Science Works only refers to past scientific work. ☐

c) **i)** How Science Works is normally taught separately. ☐

  **ii)** How Science Works is normally taught alongside the science content. ☐

  **iii)** How Science Works is not taught in the classroom. ☐

d) **i)** There will be no questions relating to How Science Works in the exam. ☐

  **ii)** There will be a separate exam covering How Science Works. ☐

  **iii)** In the exam you will need to recall facts and draw upon your knowledge of how science works. ☐

**2** Use the words below to fill the spaces and complete this list, which outlines the main areas covered by How Science Works.

| evidence | reliability | decisions | practices |
|---|---|---|---|
| explanations | procedures | validity | society |

a) The _____ and _____ used to collect scientific evidence.

b) The relationship between scientific _____ and scientific _____ and theories.

c) The _____ and _____ of scientific evidence.

d) How _____ are made about the use of science and technology.

e) The role of science in _____.

## What is the Purpose of Science?

**1** Below are ten statements about science. Read them carefully and then place a tick alongside the ones that are correct.

**a)** Scientific understanding can lead to the development of new technologies. ☐

**b)** Science looks for solutions to problems. ☐

**c)** Science is unconcerned with facts and evidence. ☐

**d)** Science tries to determine how and why things happen. ☐

**e)** Scientific knowledge has little relevance in the modern world. ☐

**f)** Scientific breakthroughs can have a huge impact on society. ☐

**g)** Scientific knowledge is only useful if you work in medicine. ☐

**h)** Science attempts to explain the world we live in. ☐

**i)** Scientific discoveries can impact on the environment. ☐

**j)** Science does not affect our everyday lives. ☐

## Scientific Evidence

**2** In your own words, describe the purpose of scientific evidence.

**3** Scientific evidence is often based on data. Name two methods of collecting data.

**a)** ............................................................................ **b)** ............................................................................

**4** It is important for scientific evidence to be reliable and valid.

**a)** What is meant by the term 'reliable'?

**b)** What is meant by the term 'valid'?

**c)** *Data can be valid, even if it is not reliable.* Is this statement **true** or **false**? ............................................................................

**d)** Why does data need to be reliable and valid?

# How Science Works

## Observations

**1** The following phrases all refer to important stages in scientific research. Number them **1** to **6**, to show the order in which they normally take place.

a) Analyse the data ☐

b) Develop a hypothesis ☐

c) Make an observation ☐

d) Amend the hypothesis ☐

e) Carry out an investigation ☐

f) Make a prediction ☐

**2 a)** Write **true** or **false**, as appropriate, alongside each of these statements about hypotheses.

i) A hypothesis summarises a number of related observations. ..............

ii) A hypothesis is a statement, which suggests an explanation for something. ..............

iii) A hypothesis is a question, which asks why a phenomenon occurs. ..............

iv) A hypothesis normally proposes a relationship between two variables. ..............

v) A hypothesis is a conclusion based on scientific data. ..............

b) What are hypotheses based on?

.............................................................................................................................

**3** What must happen if new observations, and related data, do not match existing theories and explanations relating to the same phenomenon?

.............................................................................................................................

**4** Complete the flow chart below to show the order of events that leads to a hypothesis being revised.

| hypothesis | | | | revised hypothesis |
|---|---|---|---|---|

# How Science Works

## Investigations

**1** What is the purpose of a scientific investigation?

_____

_____

**2** In a scientific investigation there are two variables: the independent variable and the dependent variable. In the space below, write a short definition for each to help you remember the difference.

**a)** Independent variable

_____

_____

**b)** Dependent variable

_____

_____

**3** A student predicts that water will evaporate at a faster rate if room temperature is increased.

For his investigation he places a beaker containing water in three different rooms. Each room is kept at a different temperature: 15°C, 20°C and 25°C.

He measures the amount of water remaining in each beaker every 24 hours.

**a)** Which is the independent variable in this investigation? Explain your answer.

_____

_____

**b)** Which is the dependent variable in this investigation? Explain your answer.

_____

_____

**c)** Is the dependent variable continuous, discrete, ordered or categoric?

_____

**d)** Identify one other variable that could affect the results of this investigation.

_____

# How Science Works

## Investigations (continued)

**4** For each example below, state whether the link between the two variables, x and y, is **causal**, **due to association**, or **due to chance.**

**a)** Variables x and y appear to be related, because an increase in x coincides with an increase in y. However, a scientific investigation finds that they are acting independently.

_____

**b)** Variables x and y both start to decrease at the same time. A scientific investigation finds that the decreases in x and y are both the result of an increase in variable z.

_____

**c)** A scientific investigation finds that a change in variable x brings about a change in variable y.

_____

**5** **a)** What is a fair test?

_____

_____

**b)** In general terms, how can you ensure a fair test?

_____

_____

**c)** Why is it often easier to achieve a fair test in laboratory conditions than in the field (e.g. when carrying out an investigation into the effects of pollutants on the environment)?

_____

_____

**6** When conducting a scientific survey, why is it important to ensure that the individuals in the sample are closely matched?

_____

_____

_____

# How Science Works

## Investigations (continued)

**7** The following passage describes how a control experiment can be used in a scientific investigation. The words **dependent**, **independent** and **data** have been deleted. Insert them into the correct spaces to complete the passage.

Scientists collect ............................ by carrying out investigations. For example, they might set up an

experiment in which they can make controlled changes to the ............................ variable and then

measure the ............................ variable.

In a control experiment, the ............................ variable is not changed, but the ............................

variable is still measured. This provides a second set of ............................ .

By comparing the two sets of ............................, the investigator can establish whether changes to the

............................ variable were caused by the ............................ variable.

If the ............................ variable shows the same changes in the control experiment, then they cannot

have been caused by the ............................ variable.

**8 a)** In an investigation, why is it a good idea to repeat the measurements and then calculate their mean?

.................................................................................................................................................................

.................................................................................................................................................................

**b)** What is the standard formula for calculating the mean of a set of values?

.................................................................................................................................................................

**c)** Calculate the mean of the following set of data (show your working).

| | Temperature (°C) |
|---|---|
| 1 | 45.2 |
| 2 | 44.8 |
| 3 | 44.7 |
| 4 | 45.0 |
| 5 | 44.7 |

**Answer:** .......................

**d)** How can the accuracy and reliability of the mean of a set of data be improved?

.................................................................................................................................................................

# How Science Works

## Measurements

**1** Name three factors that can affect the reliability and validity of measurements.

**a)** ..................................................................................................................................

**b)** ..................................................................................................................................

**c)** ..................................................................................................................................

**2** A student repeats the same measurement ten times. She notices that one of the readings is very different from the rest of the data. In your own words, explain what she should do next.

.............................................................................................................................................

.............................................................................................................................................

.............................................................................................................................................

## Presenting Data

**3** Name two benefits of presenting data in an appropriate graph or chart.

**a)** ..................................................................................................................................

**b)** ..................................................................................................................................

**4** A meteorologist measures the air temperature (in °C) every 60 minutes. What type of graph could best be used to display this data? Explain your answer.

.............................................................................................................................................

.............................................................................................................................................

## Conclusions

**5** Write **true** or **false**, as appropriate, alongside each of the following statements about scientific conclusions. Conclusions should…

**a)** include speculation and personal opinion ...................................

**b)** describe the patterns and relationships shown in the data ...................................

**c)** take all the data into account ...................................

**d)** only refer to the bits of data that support the hypothesis ...................................

**e)** make direct reference to the original hypothesis. ...................................

## Conclusions (continued)

**6** Name three points that need to be considered in an evaluation.

a) ................................................................................................................................................

b) ................................................................................................................................................

c) ................................................................................................................................................

**7** Suggest one way in which the reliability of an investigation can be improved.

................................................................................................................................................

................................................................................................................................................

**8** Use a line to connect each type of issue with the area it is concerned with.

| Social issues | | Money and resources |

| Economic issues | | Morals and value judgements |

| Environmental issues | | The human population |

| Ethical issues | | The Earth's ecosystems |

**9** **a)** List the three things you should always consider when asked to evaluate information about social-scientific issues.

i) P................................ ii) M................................ iii) I................................

**b)** Name three factors that could influence the reliability of information about social-scientific issues.

i) ................................ ii) ................................ iii) ................................

**10** *Science can answer all questions.* Is this statement **true** or **false**? Explain your answer.

................................................................................................................................................

................................................................................................................................................

................................................................................................................................................

................................................................................................................................................

# Unit 1 – 11.1

## Thermal Energy Transfer

**1** Name the three methods of transferring heat and briefly explain the differences between them.

a) ............................................................................................

b) ............................................................................................

c) ............................................................................................

**2** a) Explain why the handle of a brass poker gradually becomes hot if the other end is left in a fire.

b) What should the poker handle have on the end to stop it becoming too hot to hold? Explain your answer.

**3** Explain how a hot air balloon rises into the air.

**4** When an electric kettle is switched on it will take a few minutes to heat the water. Explain in detail how the element at the bottom of the kettle heats all of the water.

**5** a) With reference to colour and texture, which surfaces are good absorbers of radiation? ...............

b) Which surfaces are poor emitters of radiation? ...............

**6** *The shape of an object will affect how much radiation is given out or taken in by the object.* Is this statement **true** or **false**?

**7** Complete this sentence: Heat is transferred at a faster rate if…

# How Science Works

To answer the questions on this page, you will have to recall scientific facts and draw upon your knowledge of how science works, e.g. scientific procedures, issues and ideas.

**1** Name three areas in a house from which heat can easily be lost to the outside, and describe the means by which it is lost.

a) ........................................................................................................................................................

........................................................................................................................................................

b) ........................................................................................................................................................

........................................................................................................................................................

c) ........................................................................................................................................................

........................................................................................................................................................

**2** **a)** Up to 10% of heat loss is through the windows. Explain the two different insulation methods that could be used to reduce this loss, and how they work.

........................................................................................................................................................

........................................................................................................................................................

........................................................................................................................................................

**b)** Evaluate which insulation method described above you think would be the most effective, in terms of cost and stopping heat transfer.

........................................................................................................................................................

........................................................................................................................................................

........................................................................................................................................................

**3** Give one other area in the house where heat can be lost and evaluate the advantages and disadvantages of an appropriate insulating method.

........................................................................................................................................................

........................................................................................................................................................

........................................................................................................................................................

## Transferring Energy and Efficiency

**1** Explain the meaning of…

**a)** useful energy

**b)** wasted energy.

**2** List two ways in which energy is wasted by a microwave.

**a)**

**b)**

**3** Are the following statements **true** or **false**?

**a)** When devices transfer energy, energy is created.

**b)** When devices transfer energy, some of the energy is destroyed.

**4 a)** If we say that an electric drill is 60% efficient, what does this mean?

**b)** What happens to the other 40% of energy? Where does it go, and in what form?

**5** Suggest two ways in which energy could be wasted by a hairdryer.

**a)**

**b)**

# How Science Works

**To answer the questions on this page, you will have to recall scientific facts and draw upon your knowledge of how science works, e.g. scientific procedures, issues and ideas.**

**1** Describe the intended energy transfers for the following electrical devices:

**a)** Vacuum cleaner................................... **b)** Drill.................................... **c)** Cooker...................................

**2** The table below lists three everyday devices. For each one write down the 'useful' energy transfer it is designed to bring about and the way(s) in which energy is wasted.

| Device | 'Useful' Energy Transfer | 'Wasted' Energy |
|---|---|---|
| Television | | |
| Light bulb | | |
| Car | | |

**3** **a)** For every 200 joules of energy supplied to a hairdryer, only 80 joules is useful energy.

   **i)** How much energy is wasted?...................................................................................................

   **ii)** Calculate the efficiency of the hairdryer.

   ....................................................................................................................................................

**b)** For every 1000 joules of chemical energy put into a car, 760 joules are wasted. The rest is usefully transferred as kinetic energy. Calculate the efficiency of the car.

   ....................................................................................................................................................

**4** Evaluate the benefits of using an energy-efficient light bulb over a normal light bulb.

....................................................................................................................................................

....................................................................................................................................................

**5** Name another two ways in which energy consumption can be reduced around the house. Evaluate how effective they would be.

**a)** ...........................................................................................................................................

....................................................................................................................................................

**b)** ...........................................................................................................................................

....................................................................................................................................................

## Energy Transformation

**1** Why is electrical energy so useful?

.....................................................................................................................................

.....................................................................................................................................

**2** A television transforms electrical energy into sound and light energy. Name the energy transformation designed to be brought about by...

**a)** a lawn mower.........................................................................................................

**b)** a radio....................................................................................................................

**c)** an electric toothbrush..............................................................................................

**d)** an electric blanket....................................................................................................

**3** Name one other electrical device which transfers **a)** light energy and **b)** kinetic energy.

**a)** .....................................................  **b)** ...................................................

**4** What unit is power measured in?..........................................................................

**5** What unit is energy measured in?.........................................................................

**6** What two things does the energy transformed by an appliance depend on?

**a)** ................................................................................................................

**b)** ................................................................................................................

## Energy Transfer

**7** This diagram shows a system, called the National Grid, which is used for transmitting electricity all over the country.

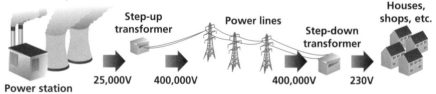

Step-up transformer    Power lines    Step-down transformer    Houses, shops, etc.

Power station    25,000V    400,000V    400,000V    230V

Describe the purpose of transformers in the National Grid.

.....................................................................................................................................

.....................................................................................................................................

.....................................................................................................................................

## Transmission of Electricity

**1 a)** How is electricity transmitted through the power lines in the National Grid? Tick the two correct answers.

**High voltage** ☐     **Low voltage** ☐     **High current** ☐     **Low current** ☐

**b)** Explain the advantages of transmitting electricity in this way.

_____

_____

**2 a)** How is electricity transmitted into homes for domestic use? Tick the two correct answers.

**High voltage** ☐     **Low voltage** ☐     **High current** ☐     **Low current** ☐

**b)** Why does the electricity need to be transmitted in this way?

_____

_____

| Electrical Device | Electric Drill | Hair Dryer | CD Player | Vacuum | Kettle | Cooker | Electric Fire |
|---|---|---|---|---|---|---|---|
| Power Rating | 600W | 500W | 160W | 1KW | 2KW | 3KW | 2KW |
| Time Switched on for | 30 secs | 10 mins | 50 mins | 5 mins | 2 mins | 30 mins | 6 hrs |
| Total Energy Transfer | | | | | | | |

## Cost of Electricity

**3** The table below shows some everyday electrical devices. Calculate the total energy transfer for each device.

**4** A rock band wants to work out the cost of the electricity that they use during one of their concerts. They know that electricity costs 8p per kilowatt hour.

For each concert they use: four speakers (750W), on for 1.5 hours (each); one smoke machine (4kW) on for 30 minutes; 20 lights (200W) on for 2 hours (each).

How much electrical energy (kWh) is transferred to power these devices during the concert?

_____

_____

# How Science Works

**To answer the questions on this page, you will have to recall scientific facts and draw upon your knowledge of how science works, e.g. scientific procedures, issues and ideas.**

**1** Bob and Lyn Davies' vacuum cleaner has broken, so they decide to go shopping for a new one. There is a large choice of vacuums with different power motors, different suction strengths, etc. The salesman in the shop pointed out three that he thought might be suitable.

A
- 10 amp motor
- non-upright
- 95 minutes of cleaning time
- £50
- Power – 1KW

B
- 10 amp motor
- upright
- full bag indicator
- 10 inch cleaning path
- £75
- Power – 1.5KW

C
- 12 amp motor
- upright
- pet friendly
- 120 minutes of cleaning time
- 15 inch cleaning path
- £80
- Power – 2KW

**a)** The Davies know that they will use their new vacuum cleaner about three times a week, for an average of 15 minutes each time. How much energy will have to be transferred to each vacuum cleaner during one week's use to do this?

A ..................................................................................................................................................

B ..................................................................................................................................................

C ..................................................................................................................................................

**b)** Compare and contrast the advantages and disadvantages of each vacuum cleaner and decide which one you would buy if you had the choice. Explain your answer.

.............................................................................................................................................................

.............................................................................................................................................................

.............................................................................................................................................................

.............................................................................................................................................................

.............................................................................................................................................................

.............................................................................................................................................................

.............................................................................................................................................................

.............................................................................................................................................................

.............................................................................................................................................................

## Non-renewable Energy Sources

**1** What is meant by the term 'fossil fuel'?

........................................................................................................................

........................................................................................................................

........................................................................................................................

**2** Name three fossil fuels.

**a)** ..............................................................................................................

**b)** ..............................................................................................................

**c)** ..............................................................................................................

**3** Explain what a 'non-renewable' energy source is.

........................................................................................................................

........................................................................................................................

........................................................................................................................

**4** Is wood considered to be a non-renewable or renewable energy source? Explain your answer.

........................................................................................................................

........................................................................................................................

........................................................................................................................

## Generating Electricity

**5** Explain how a power station using non-renewable energy sources generates electricity.

........................................................................................................................

........................................................................................................................

........................................................................................................................

........................................................................................................................

**6** Give **a)** one similarity and **b)** one difference between using nuclear and fossil fuels to generate electricity.

**a)** ..............................................................................................................

**b)** ..............................................................................................................

**7** Name two nuclear fuels.

**a)** ..............................................................................................................

**b)** ..............................................................................................................

## Comparing Non-renewable Sources of Energy

**1** Which two main pollutant gases are produced by burning fossil fuels, and what effect can they each have on the environment?

a) ........................................................................................................................................

b) ........................................................................................................................................

**2** Compare the advantages and disadvantages of using nuclear fuel over burning oil in order to produce electricity.

........................................................................................................................................

........................................................................................................................................

........................................................................................................................................

........................................................................................................................................

........................................................................................................................................

........................................................................................................................................

**3** Apart from producing pollutant gases, list another disadvantage / hazard of using gas as a fuel source.

........................................................................................................................................

**4** List two advantages of using coal to generate electricity.

a) ........................................................................................................................................

b) ........................................................................................................................................

**5** Explain why nuclear fuel has to be disposed of very carefully.

........................................................................................................................................

........................................................................................................................................

........................................................................................................................................

**6** List two general disadvantages of using non-renewable sources of energy.

a) ........................................................................................................................................

b) ........................................................................................................................................

## Renewable Energy Sources

**1** What is the main difference between using non-renewable and renewable energy in terms of generating electricity in a power station?

**2** List three renewable energy sources.

a)

b)

c)

**3** Name two renewable energy sources that would be suitable to use in Australia. Explain your answers.

a)

b)

**4** In some areas hot water and steam rise naturally to the Earth's surface.

a) What is the name given to this energy source?

b) What is the source of this energy?

**5** Electricity can be generated using a hydroelectric power station. Explain how this system can be used to store energy.

Reservoir high up

Dam

Turbines

Reservoir low down

## Comparing Renewable Energy Sources

**1** Which pollutant gases are produced by renewable energy sources?

**2** Electricity can be generated using solar energy. Describe the limitations of this method of energy production.

**3** Compare the advantages and disadvantages of using wind and hydroelectric power stations in order to produce electricity.

**4** Why do some people object to wind turbines?

**5** Give one disadvantage of using tidal and wave power to produce electricity.

**6** Give two general advantages of using renewable energy sources.

a)

b)

# How Science Works

**To answer the questions on this page, you will have to recall scientific facts and draw upon your knowledge of how science works, e.g. scientific procedures, issues and ideas.**

**1** If using fossil fuels and nuclear power to generate electricity is damaging the planet, why do we continue to use them when there are pollutant-free options? Discuss.

**2** The local council in the seaside resort of Newtown has been discussing plans to build a new power station to help cope with the increasing demand for electricity, especially during the tourist season. They have narrowed down the options to either a coal-fired power station or a wave farm built just off the coast. In the space below write a letter to the local council, expressing either your support for the wave farm, or your support for the coal-fired power station.

## Electromagnetic Spectrum

**1** What is the electromagnetic spectrum?

..................................................................................................................................................

**2 a)** Explain how the visible spectrum is produced from white light.

..................................................................................................................................................

..................................................................................................................................................

**b)** Name three practical uses of visible light.

**i)** ..........................................................................................................................................

**ii)** .........................................................................................................................................

**iii)** .......................................................................................................................................

**3** After radio waves, name the next three types of electromagnetic radiation in order of decreasing wavelength.

..................................................................................................................................................

**4** What characteristic of electromagnetic radiation determines how it is reflected, transmitted or absorbed by a particular substance?

..................................................................................................................................................

**5** When radiation is absorbed, what happens to the substance which absorbs it?

..................................................................................................................................................

**6** Write down the wave formula.

..................................................................................................................................................

**7** Are the following statements **true** or **false**?

**a)** Black surfaces are good reflectors of infra red radiation. ...................

**b)** Gamma rays, X-rays and UV rays all have a shorter wavelength compared to visible light. ...................

**c)** Radio waves, microwaves and infra red rays all have a higher frequency compared to visible light. ...................

**d)** Wavelengths with a higher frequency travel faster than those with a lower frequency. ...................

## Uses and Effects of Electromagnetic Waves

**1** List two uses of gamma rays.

**a)** ................................................................................................................

**b)** ................................................................................................................

**2** Which type of electromagnetic radiation is used… ................................................

**a)** in satellite communication networks? ................................................

**b)** in sunbeds to recreate the effects of the Sun? ................................................

**c)** in optical fibre communication? ................................................

**d)** in security coding? ................................................

**3** What are **a)** the benefits, and **b)** the dangers of using X-rays?

**a)** ................................................................................................................

**b)** ................................................................................................................

**4** What are radio waves used for?

................................................................................................................

**5** *Gamma rays can be both dangerous and beneficial to the human body.* Explain this statement.

................................................................................................................

................................................................................................................

**6 a)** Explain why frozen food can be defrosted using microwaves.

................................................................................................................

................................................................................................................

**b)** Explain why infra red rays would not be suitable for defrosting food.

................................................................................................................

................................................................................................................

## Communication Using Electromagnetic Waves

**1** **a)** Electrical signals can be sent using electromagnetic waves. Explain how an electrical signal can be transmitted from one place and then received at a different place.

**b)** What are the advantages of transmitting information via optical fibres compared to copper cables?

**2** **a)** What is the main difference between analogue and digital signals? Draw diagrams of both to help explain your answer.

**b)** List three advantages of transmitting information using digital signals rather than analogue signals.

i)

ii)

iii)

**3** Analogue signals deteriorate in quality even when they are amplified at selected intervals. Explain why.

# How Science Works

**To answer the questions on this page, you will have to recall scientific facts and draw upon your knowledge of how science works, e.g. scientific procedures, issues and ideas.**

**1 a)** What type of electromagnetic radiation is used by mobile phones?

........................................................................................................................................................................

**b)** What makes this type of radiation well-suited to mobile communication?

........................................................................................................................................................................

........................................................................................................................................................................

**c)** What are the risks generally associated with this type of radiation?

........................................................................................................................................................................

........................................................................................................................................................................

**2 a)** Name one other type of electromagnetic radiation.

........................................................................................................................................................................

**b)** Name one way in which this type of radiation can be used.

........................................................................................................................................................................

**c)** Evaluate the possible hazards of using it in this way. Do you think the benefits outweigh any dangers? Discuss.

........................................................................................................................................................................

........................................................................................................................................................................

........................................................................................................................................................................

........................................................................................................................................................................

........................................................................................................................................................................

........................................................................................................................................................................

........................................................................................................................................................................

# How Science Works

**To answer the questions on this page, you will have to recall scientific facts and draw upon your knowledge of how science works, e.g. scientific procedures, issues and ideas.**

**1 a)** Why can too much exposure to UV radiation be harmful to the human body?

_____

_____

**b)** If UV radiation is so damaging to the skin, why do we go out in the Sun? List two health benefits of being in the Sun.

**i)** _____

**ii)** _____

**2** Evaluate how effective the following methods would be in reducing exposure to UV radiation:

**a)** Wearing a baseball cap.

_____

**b)** Putting a low factor sun cream on first thing in the morning, and not reapplying.

_____

**c)** Wearing a low factor sun cream at midday.

_____

**3** Choose another type of electromagnetic radiation. List and evaluate at least two methods that can be used to reduce exposure to it.

_____

_____

_____

_____

_____

_____

_____

## Radiation

**1** Draw a simple, labelled diagram of an atom.

**2** What is meant by the term 'radioactive'?

**3** In general terms, what causes radiation to be released from an atom?

**4** What is an isotope?

**5** Match the three types of ionising radiation to the correct description with a line.

| Alpha | | High frequency radiation |
|---|---|---|
| Beta | | High energy electron from the nucleus |
| Gamma | | Helium nucleus |

**6** Of the three types of radiation, which one would be absorbed by a few millimetres of thin metal?

**7** Match the relevant properties to the correct type of radiation with a line.

| Gamma | | Easily absorbed |
|---|---|---|
| Alpha | | Poorly ionising |
| Beta | | Reasonably absorbed |

## Electric and Magnetic Fields

**1** What happens to gamma radiation in a magnetic field?

_____

_____

**2** What happens to beta radiation in an electric field?

_____

_____

**3 a)** In the diagram below, gamma radiation is being used to control the thickness of steel sheets. Explain, in as much detail as possible, how this works.

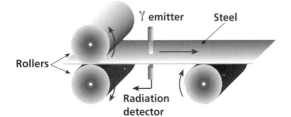

_____

_____

_____

_____

_____

_____

_____

**b)** Explain why alpha and beta radiations would not be suitable for controlling the thickness of steel.

_____

_____

**4 a)** Radiation can be used to sterilise medical instruments. What type of radiation would be used for this job?

_____

**b)** Sterile means 'free from living organisms'. How does radiation work to create sterile instruments?

_____

**5** What is a tracer?

_____

_____

## Acute Dangers

**1 a)** How does radiation create ions?

_____

_____

**b)** What effect can this ionising power have on living cells?

_____

_____

**2** Why does alpha radiation cause damage to cells if the source is inside the body?

_____

_____

**3** Why does gamma radiation cause damage to cells if the source is outside the body?

_____

_____

## Half-Life

**4 a)** What is the relationship between the amount of radiation emitted by a radioactive material and its age?

_____

**b)** What is the definition of the half-life of a radioactive isotope?

_____

_____

_____

**c)** A radioisotope with a mass of 200g has a half-life of two days. What would be the mass of the isotope after…

**i)** two days? _____

**ii)** four days? _____

**iii)** eight days? _____

# How Science Works

To answer the questions on this page, you will have to recall scientific facts and draw upon your knowledge of how science works, e.g. scientific procedures, issues and ideas.

**1** Name two types each of **a)** alpha, and **b)** beta radiation.

a) i)............................................................................ ii)............................................................................

b) i)............................................................................ ii)............................................................................

**2** What are the effects of each of the following types of radiation on human cells if they enter the body?

a) **Alpha:** ..........................................................................................................................................

b) **Beta:** ..........................................................................................................................................

c) **Gamma:** ..........................................................................................................................................

**3** If radiation is so dangerous, why do we use it? List three positive uses.

a) ..........................................................................................................................................

b) ..........................................................................................................................................

c) ..........................................................................................................................................

**4** Evaluate the benefits and hazards of using gamma radiation for treating cancer.

..................................................................................................................................................

..................................................................................................................................................

..................................................................................................................................................

..................................................................................................................................................

**5** Evaluate the benefits and hazards of using alpha radiation to treat cancer.

..................................................................................................................................................

..................................................................................................................................................

..................................................................................................................................................

..................................................................................................................................................

..................................................................................................................................................

**To answer the questions on this page, you will have to recall scientific facts and draw upon your knowledge of how science works, e.g. scientific procedures, issues and ideas.**

**1** This picture shows a worker at a nuclear plant working behind a protective screen. She works with all types of ionising radiation.

a) Name a suitable material for the screen.

_____

b) How does this screen protect her from radiation?

_____

**2** It is very important that workers in the nuclear industry do not ingest radioactive substances. What precautions can be taken to prevent this?

_____

_____

**3** Nuclear power station workers wear a special film badge to check how much radiation they have been exposed to.

a) What happens to the photographic film on exposure to radiation?

_____

b) How is the film used to find out how much radiation the person has been exposed to?

_____

c) Evaluate how effective the badge is in reducing exposure to radiation.

_____

_____

**4** Evaluate how effective it would be to wear a thin metal apron to reduce exposure to…

a) alpha radiation _____

b) beta radiation _____

c) gamma radiation. _____

# How Science Works

**To answer the questions on this page, you will have to recall scientific facts and draw upon your knowledge of how science works, e.g. scientific procedures, issues and ideas.**

**1** **a)** Radioisotopes can be used to detect leaks in pipes buried in the ground. What type of radiation would the radioisotope need to emit, and why?

......................................................................................................................................................

......................................................................................................................................................

**b)** Should the radioisotope have a long or short half-life? Explain your answer.

......................................................................................................................................................

**c)** Describe how the radioisotope is used to detect a leak in a pipe.

......................................................................................................................................................

......................................................................................................................................................

......................................................................................................................................................

**2** Evaluate the usefulness of using alpha radiation...

**a)** in medical tracers

......................................................................................................................................................

......................................................................................................................................................

**b)** to control the thickness of paper.

......................................................................................................................................................

......................................................................................................................................................

**3** Evaluate the usefulness of using beta radiation in industrial tracers.

......................................................................................................................................................

......................................................................................................................................................

**4** Evaluate the usefulness of using gamma radiation in medical tracers.

......................................................................................................................................................

......................................................................................................................................................

## Observing the Universe

**1** Why do you think it is important for scientists to be able to observe the Universe?

_____

_____

**2** Name the three main types of telescope, and for each one state the type of electromagnetic radiation it can detect.

**a)** _____

**b)** _____

**c)** _____

**3 a)** Which kind of telescope uses a parabolic dish to reflect waves?

_____

**b)** Explain how this kind of telescope works.

_____

_____

**4** Explain, in as much detail as you can, how a refracting telescope works. Draw a diagram to help explain your answer.

_____

_____

_____

## Using Telescopes

**1** **a)** List three things that can affect the quality of images in space that can be seen from a telescope based on Earth.

i)............................................... ii)............................................... iii)...............................................

**b)** What is the main advantage of using a telescope in space?

.................................................................................................................................................

## Red Shift and the Big Bang Theory

**2** **a)** Explain what red shift is.

.................................................................................................................................................

.................................................................................................................................................

.................................................................................................................................................

**b)** What does red shift tell us about other galaxies in the Universe?

.................................................................................................................................................

.................................................................................................................................................

**3** The wavelengths of light from distant galaxies are much longer than scientists would expect. What does this mean the distant galaxies are doing? Tick the correct answer.

**a)** Moving away from us slowly ☐  **b)** Moving away from us quickly ☐

**c)** Moving towards us quickly ☐  **d)** Moving towards us slowly ☐

**4** **a)** Explain what the Big Bang theory is.

.................................................................................................................................................

.................................................................................................................................................

.................................................................................................................................................

**b)** In terms of red shift, what evidence is there to support the Big Bang theory?

.................................................................................................................................................

# How Science Works

**To answer the questions on this page, you will have to recall scientific facts and draw upon your knowledge of how science works, e.g. scientific procedures, issues and ideas.**

**1** List three advantages of using a space telescope rather than a telescope based on Earth.

**a)** ...............................................................................................................................................................

**b)** ...............................................................................................................................................................

**c)** ...............................................................................................................................................................

**2** Give two advantages and two disadvantages of using **a)** refracting, and **b)** radio telescopes.

| | Advantages | Disadvantages |
|---|---|---|
| **a) Refracting** | | |
| **b) Radio** | | |

**3 a)** You have been asked to build a telescope to study our Moon. You will only need to observe the Moon when it is visible from Earth and the budget available is limited. Compare and contrast the different telescopes and decide which one you would build. Explain your answer.

...............................................................................................................................................................

...............................................................................................................................................................

...............................................................................................................................................................

...............................................................................................................................................................

**b)** What factors / problems should you be aware of when building and using your chosen telescope?

...............................................................................................................................................................

...............................................................................................................................................................

...............................................................................................................................................................

...............................................................................................................................................................

# Unit 1 – Key Words

| K | B | W | M | N | C | E | D | O | G | P | D | E | G | H | R | H | I |
|---|---|---|---|---|---|---|---|---|---|---|---|---|---|---|---|---|---|
| R | Z | J | A | T | Q | G | Q | A | J | N | C | F | N | M | N | E | S |
| Y | R | E | S | M | O | T | A | C | X | C | U | R | R | E | N | T | J |
| Q | E | L | V | D | P | I | B | T | S | C | G | Y | B | D | R | R | U |
| E | N | M | O | Q | A | R | E | H | A | L | F | L | I | F | E | E | Z |
| T | E | I | L | H | R | N | E | L | M | K | R | W | I | D | F | R | I |
| P | W | S | T | L | E | L | F | F | S | S | A | N | L | L | O | P | Y |
| K | A | X | A | R | H | E | T | E | L | E | S | C | O | P | E | P | Q |
| D | B | B | G | N | D | I | O | N | F | E | T | S | M | A | K | N | C |
| W | L | Y | E | K | B | A | A | A | W | B | C | Y | J | L | D | F | U |
| I | E | G | I | R | E | W | O | P | X | B | V | T | N | G | O | H | Z |
| C | V | O | E | P | S | Q | N | E | Q | P | T | G | I | B | P | D | S |
| K | I | L | O | W | A | T | T | H | O | U | R | T | T | O | O | P | M |
| F | A | I | A | I | T | O | J | V | X | S | Q | H | A | G | N | E | U |
| P | C | X | O | O | K | L | Y | T | Z | T | I | F | Z | R | Z | W | N |

**1** For the definitions below, find the relevant key words in the wordsearch. The answers can run horizontally, vertically, diagonally, forwards or backwards.

a) Smallest part of an element that displays the chemical properties of an element ...............................

b) The amount of electrical energy used in one hour ...............................

c) Energy sources which can be replaced ...............................

d) Another word for potential difference ...............................

e) A charged particle ...............................

f) Measured in watts ...............................

g) An instrument used for looking into space ...............................

h) Measured in joules ...............................

i) The act of a sound wave being thrown back from a surface ...............................

j) The time taken for half the atoms in radioactive material to decay ...............................

k) Flow of electrical charge ...............................

## Speed

**1** What is the definition of speed?

_____

_____

**2** What two things do you need to know to work out the speed of an object?

**a)** _____

**b)** _____

**3** A cyclist travels 60km in 2 hours. What is his average speed in kilometres per hour?

_____

## Distance–Time Graphs

**4** The distance–time graph opposite shows a cyclist's journey.

**a)** Describe the motion of the cyclist from…

**i)** O to A _____

**ii)** A to B _____

**iii)** B to C _____

**b)** What was the total distance travelled by the cyclist?

_____

**c)** How long did the journey take?

_____

**d)** Calculate the average speed of the cyclist for the first 30 minutes of the journey.

_____

## Velocity

**5** Tick the correct answer. Velocity is…

**a)** another term for speed ☐

**b)** how fast an object is accelerating ☐

**c)** a way to describe the direction an object is facing ☐

**d)** the speed and direction of travel of an object ☐

**e)** a way to describe the type of motion of an object. ☐

## Acceleration

**1** **a)** What is the definition of acceleration?

....................................................................................................................................................................

**b)** What two things do you need to know to work out the acceleration of a object?

**i)** ..............................................................................................................................................................

**ii)** .............................................................................................................................................................

**2** How is acceleration measured? Tick the correct answer.

**a)** metres per second (m/s) ☐   **b)** metres per second² (m/s²) ☐

**c)** miles per hour (mph) ☐   **d)** kilometres per hour (km/h) ☐

**3** **a)** A car accelerates uniformly from rest to a speed of 15m/s in a time of 5 seconds. Calculate the acceleration of the car.

....................................................................................................................................................................

**b)** A train accelerates from a speed of 20m/s to 34m/s in 4 seconds. Calculate the acceleration of the train.

....................................................................................................................................................................

**c)** A fighter plane travelling at a velocity of 40m/s lands on an aircraft carrier, where it stops in a time of 2 seconds. Calculate the deceleration of the plane.

....................................................................................................................................................................

## Velocity–Time Graphs

**4** The graph alongside shows a car travelling along a road.

**a)** What is the car doing for the first second?

....................................................................................................................................................................

**b)** What is the car doing for the next 4 seconds?

....................................................................................................................................................................

....................................................................................................................................................................

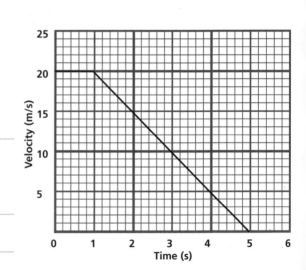

# How Science Works

**To answer the questions on this page, you will have to recall scientific facts and draw upon your knowledge of how science works, e.g. scientific procedures, issues and ideas.**

**1** An Alsatian dog, Rex, was chasing a ball in the park. His owner threw the ball 20m away and Rex ran after it for 30 seconds at a constant speed. He reached the ball and stopped for 5 seconds whilst he picked it up, before running back to his owner also at a constant speed. In the meantime however, his owner had moved 5m closer to Rex, so the dog only had to run 15m which took him 25 seconds. He dropped the ball at his owner's feet and was then stationary for a further 10 seconds before his owner threw the ball again.

Construct a distance–time graph for Rex's movements on the graph paper below.

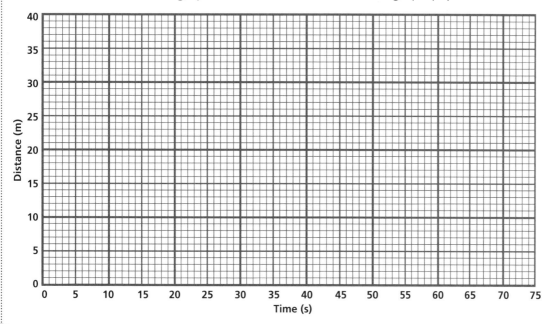

**2** The table below shows the velocity and time of a motorcyclist for the first 20 seconds of her journey.

| Velocity (m/s) | 0 | 5 | 10 | 10 | 10 | 12 | 14 | 14 | 15 | 16 | 16 |
|---|---|---|---|---|---|---|---|---|---|---|---|
| Time (s) | 0 | 2 | 4 | 6 | 8 | 10 | 12 | 14 | 16 | 18 | 20 |

Construct a velocity–time graph of the motorcyclist's journey on the graph paper below.

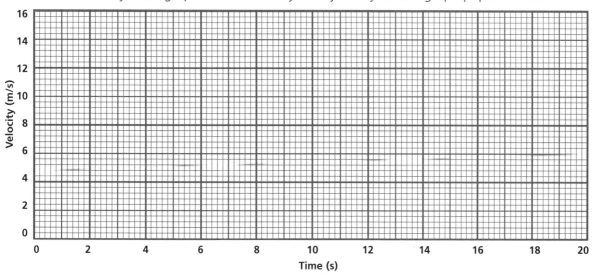

# How Science Works

**To answer the questions on this page, you will have to recall scientific facts and draw upon your knowledge of how science works, e.g. scientific procedures, issues and ideas.**

**1** The distance–time graph on the right shows Paula's shopping trip.

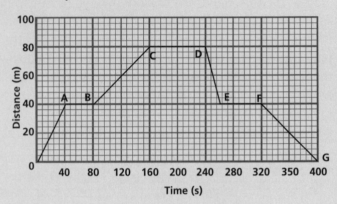

**a)** In terms of movement, describe the first 4 minutes of Paula's shopping trip.

_____

_____

_____

**b)** In which region – BC, CD, DE, EF, or FG – was she walking the fastest? _____

**c)** Calculate Paula's speed in the following regions.

    **i)** OA: _____     **ii)** BC: _____     **iii)** DE: _____

**2** The velocity–time graph below shows a train moving from one station to another.

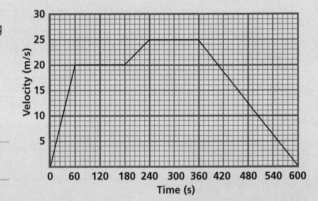

**a)** Describe the motion of the train for the first 4 minutes.

_____

_____

_____

**b)** Calculate the two accelerations of the train.

_____

_____

**c)** Calculate the deceleration of the train.

_____

**d)** Calculate the total distance travelled by the train.

_____

## Forces

**1** Complete this sentence: A stationary object exerts a downward force on the surface it rests upon. The surface exerts an upward force that is...

**2** Explain what a resultant force is.

**3** What is friction?

## Stopping Distances

**4** Tick the correct statement.

**a)** The braking distance is the stopping distance plus the thinking distance. ☐

**b)** The stopping distance is the braking distance plus the time it takes for the car to stop. ☐

**c)** The stopping distance is the thinking distance plus the braking distance. ☐

**d)** The stopping distance is the thinking distance plus the time it takes the driver to realise he needs to stop. ☐

**e)** The thinking distance is the stopping distance plus the braking distance. ☐

**5** If the overall stopping distance of a car is 56m and the thinking distance is 16m, what is the braking distance?

**6** What effect does an increase in the thinking distance have on...

**a)** the braking distance?

**b)** the overall stopping distance?

**7** List three factors that can affect the stopping distance of a car.

**a)**

**b)**

**c)**

## How Forces Affect Movement

**1** Tick the correct option to complete this sentence: If the forces acting on an object are not equal and opposite, the force is...

**a)** balanced ☐

**b)** unbalanced ☐

**c)** resultant ☐

**d)** centripetal ☐

**2** What happens to a stationary object if an unbalanced force acts on it?

........................................................................................................................................................

........................................................................................................................................................

**3** What happens to a moving object travelling at a constant speed if a balanced force acts on it?

........................................................................................................................................................

........................................................................................................................................................

**4** What happens to a moving object travelling at a constant speed if an unbalanced force acts on it?

........................................................................................................................................................

........................................................................................................................................................

**5** Nick is trying to push his car down the road, but he finds that he is unable to get the car to move by himself. He calls his dad over to help and together they push the car which starts to move and then accelerates.

**a)** Explain what would happen to the speed of the car if **i)** Nick, and then **ii)** Nick, and his dad stop pushing.

**i)** ........................................................................................................................................

........................................................................................................................................................

**ii)** ........................................................................................................................................

........................................................................................................................................................

**b)** Name the force that initially stops Nick from being able to push the car.

........................................................................................................................................................

*Weight = Mass × g*

## Force, Mass and Acceleration

*Force = Mass × Acceleration*
*F = ma*

**1** What two things does the acceleration of an object depend on?

*Size of unbalanced force*

a) *power of the car*

b) ~~(weight) of the car~~ *Mass of the car*

**2** For each of the following questions, explain your answer.

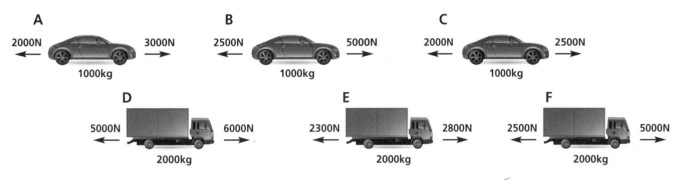

a) Which car has the smallest acceleration? *Car C* ✓

b) Which car has the greatest acceleration? *Car B* ✓

c) Which lorry has the smallest acceleration? *Lorry E* ✓

d) Which lorry has the greatest acceleration? *Lorry F*

e) Will car B or lorry F have the greatest acceleration? *Car B*

f) Which two vehicles have the same acceleration? *A and D*

**3** Write down the formula showing the relationship between mass, force and acceleration.

*Force = mass × Acceleration or F = ma*

**4** A car is moving at a constant speed of 30m/s. The combined mass of the car and the driver is 1000kg.

a) If the driving force is 3000N, what is the value of the frictional force?

*3000N*

b) If the driver increases the driving force to 4000N, calculate the acceleration of the car.

$$4000N = 1000kg × ?$$
$$F = m × a$$

$a = \dfrac{Force}{Mass}$

$a = 4 m/s^2$

**5** A motorcycle is moving along a straight road. The total mass of the motorcyclist and the bike is 250kg. The motorcyclist accelerates at 2m/s². Calculate the force needed to produce this acceleration.

*Force = mass × Acceleration*        *F = 500N*

*Force = 250kg × 2m/s² = 500N*

# Unit 2 – 12.2

## Terminal Velocity

**1 a)** Anil jumps out of a plane. He does not initially open his parachute, but freefalls towards the ground. As he is falling, he accelerates. Explain, in terms of the forces acting on Anil, why he accelerates.

*The reason why Anil accelerates is because his weight due to gravity and his downwards force is greater than the air resistance.*

**b)** What happens to the air resistance as he falls?

*The air resistance is increasing slowly to match his downward force.*

**c)** Anil will eventually stop accelerating, and will start to fall at a steady speed. Explain why this is so, and what this steady speed is called.

*The air resistance has matched his downward force and has reached his terminal velocity.*

**d)** After 40 seconds of freefall, Anil opens his parachute. What effect will this have on the air resistance acting upon him?

*It will increase*

**e)** What happens to his speed now?

*It will decrease o go to a new constant speed*

**f)** Eventually Anil will stop decelerating. Explain why.

*The air resistance will decrease when he accelerates until his weight balances the air resistance.*

**g)** Anil has reached terminal velocity twice in his jump. Will his terminal velocity be the same both times? Explain your answer.

*No because the second terminal velocity is much slower than the first one*

# How Science Works

To answer the questions on this page, you will have to recall scientific facts and draw upon your knowledge of how science works, e.g. scientific procedures, issues and ideas.

**1** As part of a training exercise, a fighter-plane pilot is required to take his plane into a steep dive, only levelling off when he reaches a certain height. The table below shows the velocity of the plane at 4 second intervals, from when the pilot first goes into the dive up until the point where he has reached the required height and pulls out of the dive.

| Velocity (km/s) | 150 | 210 | 260 | 290 | 330 | 360 | 360 | 360 |
|---|---|---|---|---|---|---|---|---|
| Time (s) | 4 | 8 | 12 | 16 | 20 | 24 | 28 | 32 |

**a)** Plot the plane's dive on the graph below.

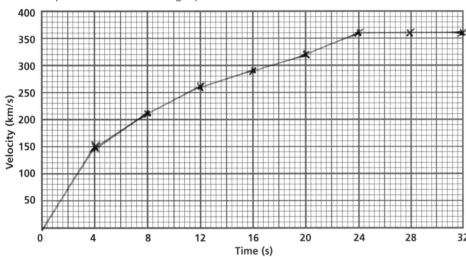

**b)** Why is the slope steeper at first?

Because he is suddenly accelerating and changing his air resistance.

**c)** What does the flat horizontal line indicate?

The pilot has reached terminal velocity.

**2 a)** Write down the formula for calculating weight.

weight = Mass × gravitational field strength or w = m × 10N/kg ✓

**b)** A number of masses are shown below. Calculate their weight on Earth, if the gravitational field strength is 10N/kg.

**i)** Mass of 2kg    2 kg × 10 = 20N ✓

**ii)** Mass of 250g    0.25 kg × 10N = 2.5 kg    0.25kg

**iii)** Mass of 10kg    10kg × 10 = 100N

**iv)** Mass of 75g    0.075 kg × 10 = 0.75N

O.075

# Unit 2 – 12.3

## Work

1. What is the relationship between work done, force and distance?

2. Tony lifts a parcel of weight 100N onto a shelf that is 2m above the ground. Calculate the work done in lifting the parcel onto the shelf.

3. Describe what elastic potential energy is.

## Kinetic Energy

4. What is kinetic energy?

5. What two things does kinetic energy depend on?

6. A truck of mass 2000kg and a car of mass 1000kg are travelling down a motorway at the same speed. Which one has the greatest kinetic energy? Explain why.

7. Two cars of the same mass are travelling down a road. Explain how one car could have more kinetic energy than the other.

HT 8. A car of mass 1000kg moves along a road at a constant speed of 20m/s. Calculate its kinetic energy.

9. A truck of mass 32 000kg moves along a road with a speed of 10m/s. Calculate its kinetic energy.

# How Science Works

**1** Name three different forms of energy that kinetic energy could be transformed into.

a) ................................................................................................................

b) ................................................................................................................

c) ................................................................................................................

**2** In the following examples, describe the form(s) of energy that kinetic energy is being transformed into.

a) A moving turbine in a power station. .................................................................

b) A falling squash ball hitting the ground. .............................................................

c) A tennis ball bouncing from the floor into the air. ..................................................

d) A car braking. ................................................................................................

e) A person bouncing on a trampoline. ...................................................................

**3** A bungee jumper, jumping off a bridge has kinetic energy. Describe how this energy is transformed when he reaches the end of the bungee cord.

................................................................................................................

................................................................................................................

................................................................................................................

**4** Can you think of another example of the transformation of kinetic energy to another form of energy? Explain how the energy would transform, the benefits of the energy transformation, and any problems created. Use the Internet, library, or another secondary source to help you.

................................................................................................................

................................................................................................................

................................................................................................................

................................................................................................................

................................................................................................................

## Momentum

**1** Does a stationary car have momentum? Explain your answer.

........................................................................................................................................

........................................................................................................................................

**2** What two things does momentum depend on?

**a)** ...............................................................................................................................

**b)** ...............................................................................................................................

**3** **a)** Write down the equation for calculating momentum.

........................................................................................................................................

**b)** Calculate the momentum of a jogger of mass 80kg running at a velocity of 0.4m/s.

........................................................................................................................................

**c)** Calculate the momentum of a car of mass 900kg travelling at a velocity of 20m/s.

........................................................................................................................................

**d)** A truck is moving with a velocity of 18m/s. Calculate its mass if it has a momentum of 61 000m/s.

........................................................................................................................................

........................................................................................................................................

## Magnitude and Direction

**4** **a)** A car of mass 1200kg is travelling at a velocity of 15m/s. What happens to its velocity and its momentum if the car then travels in the opposite direction with a speed of 15m/s?

........................................................................................................................................

........................................................................................................................................

**b)** Calculate the momentum of the car when it travels in the opposite direction.

........................................................................................................................................

........................................................................................................................................

## Force and Change in Momentum

**1** In terms of momentum, what happens when an unbalanced force acts on a stationary object?

**2** What two things can happen to momentum when an unbalanced force acts on a moving object?

a)

b)

**3** The extent of change in momentum depends on two factors. What are they?

a)

b)

**HT** **4** How can change in momentum be calculated?

**5** Jenny is playing squash. The ball is coming towards her at a momentum of 5kg m/s. She swings with a force that acts on the ball for 0.9 seconds and the ball then speeds off towards the front wall with a momentum of 10kg m/s.

a) What is the change in momentum of the ball?

b) With what force did Jenny's racket hit the ball?

c) How could Jenny increase the momentum and velocity of the ball, without increasing the force applied?

## Collisions and Explosions

**1** In a collision or explosion, momentum is conserved. What does this mean?

_____

_____

**2** Two cars are travelling in the same direction along a road. Car A collides with car B and they lock together. Calculate their velocity after the collision.

BEFORE:  A  12m/s  B  10m/s  AFTER:  A  B  → v
1000kg  1200kg

_____

_____

_____

**3** Two cars are travelling towards each other along a road. Car A collides with car B and they stick together. Calculate their velocity after the collision.

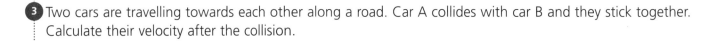

BEFORE:  A  12m/s 5m/s  B  AFTER:  A  B  → v
1000kg  800kg

_____

_____

_____

**4** A gun is fired as below. If the recoil velocity of the gun is 2m/s, calculate the velocity of the bullet.

BEFORE:  AFTER:  2m/s ←  0.005kg → v

1.5kg

_____

_____

_____

_____

# How Science Works

**To answer the questions on this page, you will have to recall scientific facts and draw upon your knowledge of how science works, e.g. scientific procedures, issues and ideas.**

**1 a)** In terms of momentum, what happens to a passenger in the front of a car if the car crashes and comes to a sudden halt and he/she is not wearing a seat belt?

.......................................................................................................................................

.......................................................................................................................................

**b)** In terms of momentum, how does a seat belt work?

.......................................................................................................................................

.......................................................................................................................................

.......................................................................................................................................

**2** In terms of momentum, explain how a crumple zone in a car works.

.......................................................................................................................................

.......................................................................................................................................

.......................................................................................................................................

**3** Name one other safety feature in a car that is concerned with momentum and explain how it works.

.......................................................................................................................................

.......................................................................................................................................

.......................................................................................................................................

.......................................................................................................................................

.......................................................................................................................................

.......................................................................................................................................

.......................................................................................................................................

.......................................................................................................................................

## Static Electricity

**1 a)** The picture opposite shows Paula charging a balloon with static electricity. Explain how the balloon gains a positive charge.

.......................................................................................................................

.......................................................................................................................

**b)** What charge will Paula's jumper have?

.......................................................................................................................

**2** Thomas was in a classroom at school where there was a nylon carpet on the floor. He found that if he walked across the classroom and touched a metal radiator he got an electric shock. Explain why.

.......................................................................................................................

.......................................................................................................................

## Repulsion and Attraction

**3** An ebonite rod is moved near to a second ebonite rod which is suspended on a string. What will happen to the suspended rod? Explain your answer.

.......................................................................................................................

**4** An ebonite rod is moved near to a suspended Perspex rod. What will happen to the suspended rod? Explain your answer.

.......................................................................................................................

## Uses of Static

**5** Give two examples of how static electricity can be used in everyday life.

**a)** ...........................................................  **b)** ..........................

**6** Explain how a smoke precipitator works using electrostatic charges.

.......................................................................................................................

.......................................................................................................................

.......................................................................................................................

.......................................................................................................................

## Uses of Static (cont.)

**1** The following mixed-up statements describe how a photocopier works.

**a)** ... charged impression of the plate attracts tiny specs of black powder...

**b)** ... paper is heated to fix the final image...

**c)** ... copying plate is electrically charged...

**d)** ... powder is transferred from the plate to the paper...

**e)** ... image of the page to be copied is projected onto the plate...

**f)** ... charge leaks away due to light, leaving an electrostatic impression of page...

Write down the correct order in which the statements should appear.

☐ ☐ ☐ ☐ ☐ ☐

## Discharge of Static Electricity

**2** Static electricity can be discharged. Explain what this means.

**3** Why are metals good conductors of electricity?

**4** Explain how a conductor, attached to a positively charged dome, discharges electricity.

**HT**

**5** What causes electricity to flow though the air?

**6** How is the energy flow in a conductor attached to a negatively charged dome different to one attached to a positively charged dome?

# How Science Works

To answer the questions on this page, you will have to recall scientific facts and draw upon your knowledge of how science works, e.g. scientific procedures, issues and ideas.

**1** Why is it important to ensure that static electricity is discharged safely?

.......................................................................................................................................

.......................................................................................................................................

**2** During the refuelling of planes, care needs to be taken to avoid dangerous electrical discharges.

    **a)** Why could there be a discharge?

       .......................................................................................................

       .......................................................................................................

    **b)** Explain how this discharge can be made safe.

       .......................................................................................................

       .......................................................................................................

**3** **a)** Explain why static electricity is a real hazard at a petrol station.

       .......................................................................................................

       .......................................................................................................

    **b)** Give two precautions that should be taken at a petrol station to avoid the discharge of static electricity.

       **i)** ..............................................................................................

       **ii)** .............................................................................................

**4** **a)** Explain how computers can be damaged by static electricity.

       .......................................................................................................

       .......................................................................................................

    **b)** What precaution can computer technicians take to avoid damaging computers with static electricity? Explain your answer.

       .......................................................................................................

       .......................................................................................................

# How Science Works

**5** What is lightning?

........................................................................................................

........................................................................................................

........................................................................................................

**6** Explain how a lightning conductor protects a building from lightning.

........................................................................................................

........................................................................................................

........................................................................................................

........................................................................................................

**7** During a thunderstorm, explain why it can be dangerous to…

**a)** stand under a tree

........................................................................................................

........................................................................................................

**b)** hold an umbrella with a metal tip

........................................................................................................

........................................................................................................

........................................................................................................

**c)** stand in the middle of a field.

........................................................................................................

........................................................................................................

........................................................................................................

**8** Some people attach a strip of rubber to their car, which extends to the ground, to help avoid electric shocks. In theory, how could this help?

........................................................................................................

........................................................................................................

........................................................................................................

........................................................................................................

........................................................................................................

## Circuits

**1** Below are five simple circuits (all the cells and lamps are identical).

   **a)** Which circuit has the greatest potential difference?

   **b)** Which circuit has the least potential difference?

   **c)** Which circuit has the greatest resistance?

   **d)** Which circuit has the least resistance?

**2** Which circuit would have the brightest lamp(s)? Explain why.

**3** Which circuit would have the dimmest lamp(s)? Explain why.

**4** Which two circuits have the same current flowing through them? Explain why.

## Potential Difference and Current

**5** What unit is potential difference measured in?

**6** What unit is current measured in?

## Resistance

**1** What is the definition of resistance in a circuit?

.................................................................................................................................................

**2** How are potential difference, current and resistance related?

.................................................................................................................................................

**3** For the circuits shown below, each cell provides a potential difference of 1.5V. For each circuit calculate

**a)**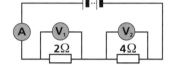

**b)**

**c)**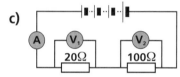

**i)** ................................................

**i)** ................................................

**i)** ................................................

**ii)** ...............................................

**ii)** ...............................................

**ii)** ...............................................

**iii)** ..............................................

**iii)** ..............................................

**iii)** ..............................................

**iv)** ..............................................

**iv)** ..............................................

**iv)** ..............................................

**i)** the potential difference supplied, **ii)** the total resistance, **iii)** the ammeter reading, and **iv)** $V_1$ and $V_2$

## Resistance of Components

**4** Below are three current–potential difference graphs. Which graph corresponds to the following components?

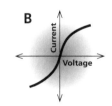

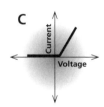

**a)** A diode. ................................................

**b)** A resistor at a constant temperature. ................................................

**c)** A filament lamp. ................................................

**5** Name the component…

**a)** whose resistance decreases as the light intensity on it increases ................................

**b)** which allows a current to flow through it in one direction only ................................

## Series and Parallel Circuits

**1** For each circuit shown below, write the missing values for current and potential difference in the spaces provided (the lamps in each circuit are identical). All bulbs have equal resistance.

**A**
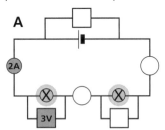

**B**
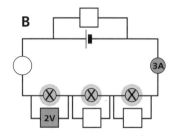

**C**
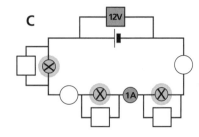

**D**
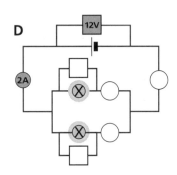

**E**
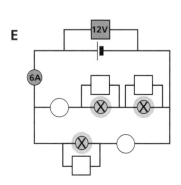

**F**
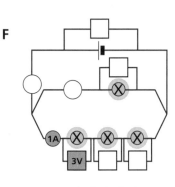

**2** In the series circuit shown opposite each cell provides a p.d. of 1.5V.

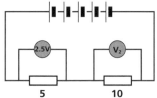

**a)** What is the total resistance of the circuit?.........................................

**b)** What is the p.d. across the 10Ω resistor?.........................................

**3** For the parallel circuit shown opposite, answer the following:

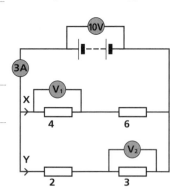

**a)** What is the total resistance of branch X of the circuit? .........................

**b)** What is the total resistance of branch Y of the circuit? .........................

**c)** What is the current through…

  **i)** branch X? .........................................

  **ii)** branch Y? .........................................

**d)** The potential difference of the supply is 10V.

  **i)** What is the value of the p.d, $V_1$? .........................................

  **ii)** What is the value of the p.d, $V_2$? .........................................

To answer the questions on this page, you will have to recall scientific facts and draw upon your knowledge of how science works, e.g. scientific procedures, issues and ideas.

**1** For each of the following electrical symbols write down the name of the component it represents.

a)    b)    c)    d)

......................    ......................    ......................    ......................

**2** Draw the symbols for these electrical components.

**a)** Battery....................    **b)** Variable Resistor....................    **c)** Thermistor....................    **d)** Switch (closed)....................

**3** In the space provided, draw a circuit diagram to represent the circuit (below). Include on your diagram...

**a)** an open switch; **b)** an ammeter to measure the current; **c)** a voltmeter to measure the p.d across the cells.

## Applying Circuit Diagrams to Practical Solutions

**4** Name one example of a simple circuit that is used in an everyday situation. Explain how the circuit is used and draw a circuit diagram to explain your answer.

## Currents

**1** How does an alternating current differ from a direct current?

........................................................................................................................

........................................................................................................................

**2** What is the voltage of UK mains electricity? Tick the correct answer.

**a)** 235V ☐          **b)** 230V ☐

**c)** 240V ☐          **d)** 245V ☐

## The Three-Pin Plug

**3** Name three everyday electrical appliances that are connected to the mains electricity supply.

**a)** ................................ **b)** ................................ **c)** ................................

**4 a)** Complete the diagram of the 3-pin plug by adding the correct wires, cables and connections. Label all the parts, including what colours the different wires should be.

**b)** What is the casing made of, and why?

........................................................................................................................

**c)** What are the inner cores of the wires made of, and why?

........................................................................................................................

**d)** What are the pins in the plug made of, and why?

........................................................................................................................

**HT** **5 a)** What kind of voltages does the live wire vary between?

........................................................................................................................

**b)** What voltage is the neutral wire always close to?

........................................................................................................................

## Circuit Breakers and Fuses

**1** What is the purpose of a circuit breaker or a fuse?

_____

**2** Explain how a circuit breaker works.

_____

_____

_____

**3** Explain how a fuse works.

_____

_____

_____

_____

**4** Are there any advantages to using a circuit breaker rather than a fuse?

_____

_____

_____

## Earthing

**5** In a metal toaster, the earth wire is connected to the outer casing of the toaster.

**a)** If the brown live wire became loose and touched the outer casing of the toaster, how would the earth wire make the appliance safe?

_____

_____

_____

**b)** What two things together protect the toaster and the user?

_____

_____

# How Science Works

To answer the questions on this page, you will have to recall scientific facts and draw upon your knowledge of how science works, e.g. scientific procedures, issues and ideas.

**1** For the 3-pin plug shown opposite, write down four faults.

a) .................................................................................................

b) .................................................................................................

c) .................................................................................................

d) .................................................................................................

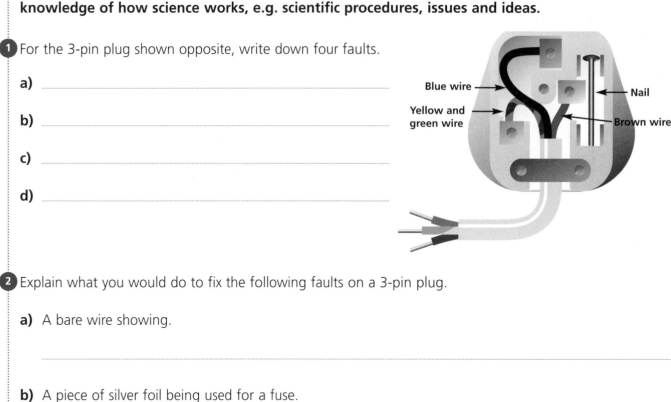

Blue wire ——→

Yellow and green wire ——→

←—— Nail

←—— Brown wire

**2** Explain what you would do to fix the following faults on a 3-pin plug.

a) A bare wire showing.

.................................................................................................

b) A piece of silver foil being used for a fuse.

.................................................................................................

c) A loose cable grip.

.................................................................................................

d) A frayed cable.

.................................................................................................

**3** Explain why you should never touch a socket with wet hands.

.................................................................................................

.................................................................................................

.................................................................................................

**4** Why should you never overload a plug socket?

.................................................................................................

.................................................................................................

To answer the questions on this page, you will have to recall scientific facts and draw upon your knowledge of how science works, e.g. scientific procedures, issues and ideas.

**1** Three traces from an oscilloscope screen are shown below.

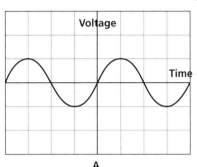 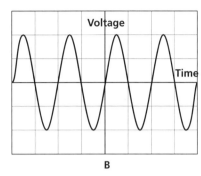 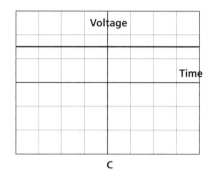

A                B                C

**a)** Which of the three traces shows a direct current?

_____

**b)** If the peak voltage on trace A is 5V, what is the peak voltage of trace B?

_____

**c)** If the frequency of trace B is 50Hz, what is the frequency of trace A?

_____

**2** Look at trace A in Question 1. On the screen below sketch a trace of an alternating current which is half the frequency, and three times the voltage, of trace A.

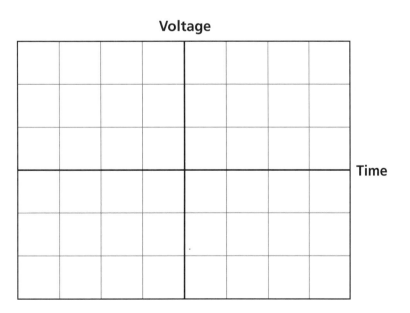

## Power

**1 a)** What is an electric current?

_____

**b)** What unit is used to measure electric currents?

_____

**2** Write down the equation by which power, potential difference and current are related.

_____

**3** An electric motor works at a current of 3A and a potential difference of 24V. What is the power of the motor?

_____

**4** A 4W light bulb works at a current of 2A. What is the potential difference?

_____

**HT**

**5** How is charge calculated?

_____

**6** How is energy transformation calculated?

_____

**7** In the circuit below, the lamp is switched on for 5 minutes and the reading on the ammeter is 3A. Calculate…

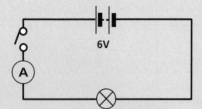

6V

A

**a)** the charge that flows _____

**b)** the energy transformed _____

**c)** the power of the lamp in the circuit. _____

# How Science Works

To answer the questions on this page, you will have to recall scientific facts and draw upon your knowledge of how science works, e.g. scientific procedures, issues and ideas.

**1 a)** Why do fuses come in different sizes?

...........................................................................................................................

**b)** What would happen if you used a 3A fuse for a device that was running on a 13V current?

...........................................................................................................................

...........................................................................................................................

...........................................................................................................................

**c)** What would happen if you used a 13A fuse for a device that was running on a 2V current?

...........................................................................................................................

...........................................................................................................................

...........................................................................................................................

**2** What is the formula for working out the current of an appliance?

...........................................................................................................................

...........................................................................................................................

**3** It is important that electrical appliances are fitted with the correct size of fuse. In the table below, work out the normal working current for each appliance and state the correct fuse needed for each appliance.

| Appliance | Power rating (W) | P.D. (V) | Working current | Fuse size (1A, 3A, 5A, 13A) |
|---|---|---|---|---|
| Iron | 920 | 230 | | |
| Kettle | 2300 | 230 | | |
| Hi-fi | 80 | 240 | | |
| Vacuum | 1400 | 230 | | |
| Toaster | 720 | 240 | | |

**4** Katy buys a brand new microwave with a power rating of 850W and potential difference of 230V. Calculate the size of the fuse required for the appliance.

...........................................................................................................................

## Atoms

**1** Why does an atom have no overall charge?

_____

_____

**2** *An electron has a negative mass.* Is this statement **true** or **false**?

_____

**3** If you know the number of protons in an atom, is it possible to deduce how many electrons there are? Explain your answer.

_____

_____

**4** Tick the statement that provides the best definition for an isotope.

**a)** Atoms of the same element with a different number of protons ☐

**b)** Atoms of the same element with a different number of neutrons ☐

**c)** Atoms of a different element with the same number of neutrons ☐

**d)** The number of protons in an element ☐

**5** What is the mass number of an element?

_____

## Ionisation

**6 a)** What is an ion?

_____

**b)** How can radioactive particles create ions?

_____

**7** Name two types of ionising radiation.

**a)** _____

**b)** _____

## Radioactive Decay and Background Radiation

**8** What is radioactive decay?

_____

_____

_____

**9** Explain how beta radiation is formed.

_____

_____

_____

_____

**10** Why is gamma radiation different from alpha and beta radiation?

_____

_____

_____

**11** Explain why there is radiation all around us, and give two examples of where this kind of radiation comes from.

_____

_____

_____

**12** Draw an accurate pie chart in the space below to show the proportions of radiation from man-made sources compared to that from natural sources.

# How Science Works

To answer the questions on this page, you will have to recall scientific facts and draw upon your knowledge of how science works, e.g. scientific procedures, issues and ideas.

**1 a)** Who came up with the 'plum pudding' model of the atom, and what theory did he propose?

_____

_____

**b)** Sketch a labelled diagram of the plum pudding model.

```
┌─────────────────────────────────────────────────────────┐
│                                                           │
│                                                           │
│                                                           │
│                                                           │
│                                                           │
│                                                           │
└─────────────────────────────────────────────────────────┘
```

**2** What experiment did Ernest Rutherford design in 1911? _____

**3 a)** Describe, in as much detail as possible, what Rutherford did in his experiment.

_____

_____

_____

**b)** Explain what happened to the alpha particles in the experiment.

_____

_____

**c)** Explain why some of the particles were deflected back towards the source.

_____

_____

**4** What conclusions on the structure of the atom did Rutherford draw from his experiment?

_____

_____

_____

## Nuclear Fusion and Fission

**1** Explain the difference between nuclear fission and nuclear fusion.

_____

_____

**2 a)** What happens during nuclear fusion?

_____

_____

**b)** What is produced during nuclear fusion?

_____

**3** Why is nuclear fusion a self-sustaining reaction?

_____

**4** Explain how the Sun produces light and heat energy.

_____

_____

**5** Name two substances commonly used in nuclear fission.

**a)** _____

**b)** _____

**6** Nuclear fission can be used on a large scale in a nuclear reactor. Once fission has started it continues by itself. Explain why.

_____

_____

_____

_____

## Nuclear Fusion and Fission (continued)

**7** The diagram below shows small-scale nuclear fission. Write the following labels in the correct places on the diagram.

**Energy**                    **New radioactive nuclei are formed**                    **Uranium nucleus**

**Further neutrons**          **Neutron**          **Unstable nucleus, fissions occurs and nucleus splits**

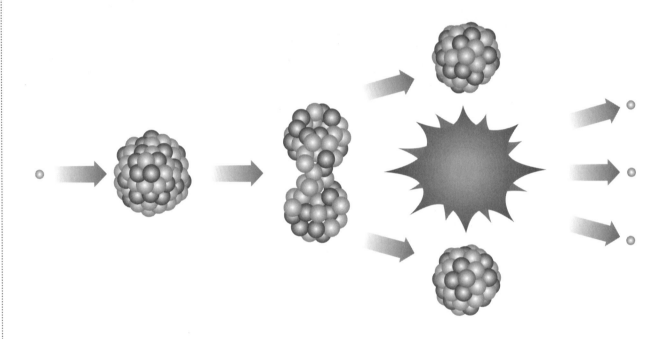

**8 a)** What are the products of nuclear fission?

    **i)** ........................................................................................................................

    **ii)** ........................................................................................................................

**b)** Are these products **radioactive** or **non-radioactive**?

........................................................................................................................

**c)** What potential problem does this pose?

........................................................................................................................

........................................................................................................................

**1** Fill in the crossword using the following clues below:

**Across**

**1)** A constant falling speed (8,8)

**6)** How fast an object is travelling (5)

**8)** Can be either direct or alternating (7)

**10)** Atoms of the same element with different numbers of neutrons (7)

**11)** The type of electricity you would create if you rubbed your hair with a balloon (6)

**12)** The amount of matter in a body (4)

**14)** What happens when two like charges come together? (9)

**16)** A neutrally charged subatomic particle (7)

**17)** Allows current to flow in one direction only (5)

**Down**

**1)** A resistor that is affected by changes in temperature (10)

**2)** A state of motion (8)

**3)** Measured in joules (6)

**4)** A device which trips a circuit (7-7)

**5)** A measure of force (6)

**7)** A resistive force (8)

**9)** A negatively charged subatomic particle (8)

**13)** A positively charged subatomic particle (6)

**15)** Charged particles (4)

## Moments

**1** What is a 'moment'?

_____

**2** A spanner is being used to unscrew a nut. Give two ways of increasing the moment of the spanner.

**a)** _____

**b)** _____

**3** **a)** Write down the equation for working out the size of the moment.

_____

**b)** Complete the following table:

| Force | Perpendicular distance between line of action and pivot | Moment |
|---|---|---|
| 10N | 0.2m | |
| 20N | | 5Nm |
| | 80cm | 12Nm |
| 1.6N | | 0.08Nm |
| 0.5N | 1200mm | |

## Centre of Mass

**4** What is meant by the centre of mass of an object?

_____

_____

**5** With a symmetrical object, where would the centre of mass be found?

_____

**6** Explain how you would find the centre of mass of a piece of paper using a plumbline.

_____

_____

_____

_____

## Law of Moments

**1** According to the law of moments, tick the correct statement.
If an object is balanced…

**a)** total clockwise moments are greater than total anticlockwise moments ☐

**b)** total anticlockwise moments are greater than total clockwise moments ☐

**c)** total clockwise moments are equal to total anticlockwise moments ☐

**d)** force is equal to weight ☐

**2** The diagram alongside shows the forces acting on a balanced object. It is pivoted at its centre of mass. Calculate $F_1$.

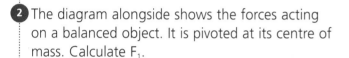

...................................................................................................

...................................................................................................

...................................................................................................

...................................................................................................

**3** The diagram alongside shows the forces acting on a balanced object. Calculate the weight, W, of the object.

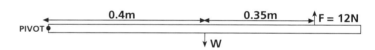

...................................................................................................

...................................................................................................

...................................................................................................

## Stability

**4** Why does an object topple over?

...................................................................................................

...................................................................................................

**5** What two things could increase the stability of a double-decker bus?

**a)** ...................................................................................................

**b)** ...................................................................................................

## Circular Motion and Centripetal Force

**1** Give three examples of objects that travel in circular or near circular paths.

**a)** ....................................................................................................................................................

**b)** ....................................................................................................................................................

**c)** ....................................................................................................................................................

**2** When an object moves in a circle, it continuously accelerates towards the centre of the circle. What does this acceleration change? Tick the correct answer.

**a)** The speed of the object ☐          **b)** The force of the object ☐

**c)** The velocity of the object ☐          **d)** The direction of motion of the object ☐

**3 a)** What is centripetal force?

.................................................................................................................................................................

.................................................................................................................................................................

**b)** Name three forces that can work in this way.

**i)** ..............................................  **ii)** ..............................................  **iii)** ..............................................

**4** Look at diagram A alongside. Under each of the following diagrams explain, in comparison to diagram A, what is happening to the centripetal force, and why.

**a)** .........................................................................................................................

.................................................................................................................................................................

**b)** .........................................................................................................................

.................................................................................................................................................................

**c)** .........................................................................................................................

.................................................................................................................................................................

## Gravity and our Solar System

**1** Explain, in terms of centripetal force, what keeps the Earth and other planets in orbit around the Sun, and stops them from drifting off into space.

_____

_____

_____

**2** Why do objects need to orbit at particular speeds?

_____

_____

_____

**3** As the distance between two objects increases, what happens to the force of gravity between them? Tick the correct answer.

**a)** It increases ☐       **b)** It stays the same ☐

**c)** It decreases ☐       **d)** It depends on the size of the objects ☐

## Artificial Satellites

**4** The diagram alongside shows a satellite which orbits the Earth once every 24 hours.

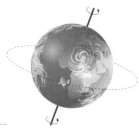

**a)** What is the name given to this type of orbit?

_____

**b)** Suggest an artificial satellite which might be put into this type of orbit, and explain why it would be suitable.

_____

**c)** Explain why there can only be a limited number of these types of satellites in this orbit.

_____

**5** The diagram alongside shows a satellite which orbits the Earth once every 90 minutes.

**a)** What is the name given to this type of orbit?

_____

**b)** Suggest an artificial satellite which might be put into this type of orbit, and why it would be suitable.

_____

# How Science Works

**To answer the questions on this page, you will have to recall scientific facts and draw upon your knowledge of how science works, e.g. scientific procedures, issues and ideas.**

**1** The diagram below shows the nine planets closest to the Sun in our Solar System.

**a)** Which planet has the longest orbiting time?

_____

**b)** Which planet has the shortest orbiting time?

_____

**2** Using the information below, complete the table to show what type of orbit the satellites are in.

| Information on Satellite | Type of Orbit (Geostationary or Polar) |
|---|---|
| Orbital period exactly matches the Earth | |
| Takes 24 hours to orbit | |
| Used to send radio and TV signals from one country to another | |
| Takes 250 minutes to orbit | |
| Appears to be in a fixed point above the Earth | |
| Used to monitor the movements of clouds | |

## Reflection of Light

**1** What is an incident ray?

....................................................................................................................................................

**2** What is a reflected ray?

....................................................................................................................................................

**3** What is the normal line used to calculate?

....................................................................................................................................................

**4** Draw a fully labelled diagram to show the reflection of a ray of light off a plane mirror, if it strikes the surface of the mirror at a 45° angle.

## Refraction of Light

**5** What is the difference between reflection and refraction?

....................................................................................................................................................

....................................................................................................................................................

**6 a)** The diagram opposite shows two rays of light striking a perspex block. Complete the paths of the rays through the block and out again.

**b)** Explain why the rays behave in the way that your completed diagram shows.

....................................................................................................................................................

....................................................................................................................................................

....................................................................................................................................................

## Internal Reflection and Prisms

**1** An experiment was carried out where the passage of a ray of light through a semi-circular block was drawn at different angles of incidence. The angles of refraction and reflection were measured for each ray of light. The results were as follows:

| Ray | Angle of Incidence | Angle of Refraction | Angle of Reflection |
|-----|--------------------|---------------------|---------------------|
| 1 | 10° | 15° | 10° |
| 2 | 20° | 31° | 19° |
| 3 | 30° | 49° | 31° |
| 4 | 40° | 75° | 40° |
| 5 | 50° | n/a | 51° |
| 6 | 60° | n/a | 60° |
| 7 | 70° | n/a | 70° |
| 8 | 80° | n/a | 81° |

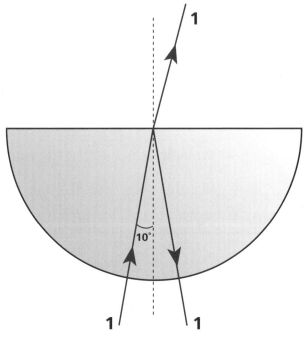

**a)** Complete the diagram from the information in the table above. Ray 1 has been drawn for you.

**b)** **i)** Rays 5–8 have not been refracted but only reflected. What is this kind of reflection called?

_____

**ii)** Explain why the rays were not refracted.

_____

**2** What happens to light travelling through a prism?

_____

**3** What is an image? Tick the correct answer.

**a)** Another word for an object ☐

**b)** A representation of an object ☐

**c)** An upside-down object ☐

**d)** Something we can only see in a mirror ☐

## Images Produced by Mirrors

**1** Explain the difference between a virtual image and a real image.

_____

_____

**2** Explain, in terms of curvature, the difference between a plane, convex and concave mirror.

_____

**3** Tick the answer which best describes what the focus point is.

a) The point to which rays are refracted ☐

b) The point from which rays appear to be refracted ☐

c) The point to which rays are reflected ☐

d) The point where all the light is focused ☐

**4** Describe the kind of image you would get from a plane mirror.

_____

**5 a)** Describe the kind of image you would get from a convex mirror.

_____

**b)** Give an example for the use of a convex mirror.

_____

**6 a)** Explain how you can get both real and virtual images from a concave mirror. What determines the kind of image you get?

_____

_____

_____

_____

**b)** Give an example for the use of a concave mirror.

_____

## Images Produced by Lenses

**1** Which of the following statements best describes a converging lens?

**a)** Thinnest at its centre and the image can be real or virtual ☐

**b)** Thickest at its centre and the image can be real or virtual ☐

**c)** Thickest at its centre and the image is nearly always virtual ☐

**d)** Light is refracted outwards by the lens ☐

**2** Which of the following statements best describes a diverging lens?

**a)** Thinnest at its centre and the image is always virtual ☐

**b)** Thickest at its centre and the image is always virtual ☐

**c)** Thinnest at its centre and the image can be real or virtual ☐

**d)** Light is refracted inwards ☐

**3 a)** What happens to rays of light as they pass though…

**i)** a converging lens?

**ii)** a diverging lens?

**b)** Are there any light rays which are the exception to the above? If so, which one(s)?

**4** What kind of image is formed by a diverging lens?

**5** Which of the following statements best describes the image formed by a camera?

**a)** The image is larger than the object and nearer to the lens ☐

**b)** The image is smaller than the object and nearer to the lens ☐

**c)** The image is larger than the object and further from the lens ☐

**d)** The image is smaller than the object and further from the lens ☐

# How Science Works

To answer the questions on this page, you will have to recall scientific facts and draw upon your knowledge of how science works, e.g. scientific procedures, issues and ideas.

**1** A scientist uses a magnifying lens to examine a piece of fibre. The fibre is 0.8mm wide. Calculate the magnification of the lens needed to produce an image of the magnified fibre which is 5.6mm wide.

................................................................................................................................................................

**2** What can ray diagrams tell us about an image?

................................................................................................................................................................

**3** **a)** Draw a ray diagram for a concave mirror where the object is the same distance from F as F is from the mirror.

**b)** Describe what kind of image is produced. ................................................................................................

**4** What type of lens is used in a magnifying glass? Explain how it works.

................................................................................................................................................................

................................................................................................................................................................

................................................................................................................................................................

**5** **a)** Draw a ray diagram for a diverging lens when the object is located just beyond F.

**b)** Describe what kind of image is produced.

................................................................................................................................................................

# How Science Works

## (cont.)

**6 a)** Draw a ray diagram for a converging lens when the object is at F.

**b)** Describe what kind of image is produced.

**7** The following questions are all about converging lenses. Tick the correct answers.

**a)** When the object is beyond 2F, what kind of image is produced?

**i)** Real, right way up and bigger ☐     **ii)** Real, upside down and bigger ☐

**iii)** Real, right way up and smaller ☐     **iv)** Real, upside down and smaller ☐

**b)** When an object is at 2F, what kind of image is produced?

**i)** Real, right way up and smaller ☐     **ii)** Real, upside down and bigger ☐

**iii)** Real, upside down and same size as object ☐     **iv)** Real, right way up and same size as object ☐

**c)** When the image is between 2F and F, what kind of image is produced?

**i)** Real, upside down and smaller ☐     **ii)** Real, the right way up and bigger ☐

**iii)** Real, the right way up and smaller ☐     **iv)** Real, upside down and bigger ☐

**d)** When the object is between F and the lens, what kind of image is produced?

**i)** Virtual, the right way up and bigger ☐     **ii)** Virtual, upside down and smaller ☐

**iii)** Virtual, upside down and bigger ☐     **iv)** Virtual, the right way up and smaller ☐

## Sound

**1** How is sound produced?

..................................................................................................................................................

**2** Between which frequencies can sound be heard by the human ear?

..................................................................................................................................................

**3 a)** How does sound travel? Give two examples that provide evidence of this.

**i)** ...........................................................................................................................................

**ii)** ..........................................................................................................................................

**b)** Explain why the person shown in the diagram below would be able to hear the plane even though he cannot see it. (You can draw on the diagram to help explain your answer.)

..........................................................................

..........................................................................

..........................................................................

..........................................................................

..........................................................................

**4 a)** What determines the frequency of a sound?

..................................................................................................................................................

**b)** If the frequency of a sound is decreased, what happens to the pitch?

..................................................................................................................................................

**5 a)** Explain what is meant by amplitude.

..................................................................................................................................................

**b)** What happens to the volume of sound as the amplitude increases?

..................................................................................................................................................

# How Science Works

**To answer the questions on this page, you will have to recall scientific facts and draw upon your knowledge of how science works, e.g. scientific procedures, issues and ideas.**

**1** The diagrams show the traces of five different notes on an oscilloscope screen.

a) Which of the traces A to E shows…

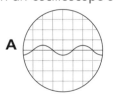     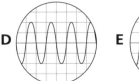 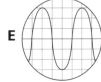

**i)** the largest amplitude? ........................................

**ii)** the highest frequency? ........................................

**iii)** the quietest sound? ........................................

**iv)** the lowest pitch? ........................................

b) Which three notes have the same pitch but different loudness?

........................................................................................................................

c) Which two notes have the same loudness but different pitch?

........................................................................................................................

d) Which note is twice as loud as the note on trace A? ........................................

e) Which note is half as loud as the note on trace D? ........................................

f) Which note has twice the pitch of the note on trace C? ........................................

g) Which note has a third of the pitch of the note on trace D? ........................................

**2** The diagrams below show the traces of two different notes, A (Grid 1) and B (Grid 2).

a) Which is the loudest note? Explain your answer.

........................................................................

........................................................................

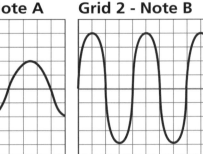

Grid 1 - Note A    Grid 2 - Note B

b) Which is the lowest pitched note? Explain your answer.

........................................................................

........................................................................

c) On grid 1 draw the trace you would expect to see for a note whose loudness and pitch are double that of note A.

d) On grid 2 draw the trace you would expect to see for a note whose loudness is a quarter, and pitch a half, of note B.

## Ultrasound

**1** What is ultrasound, and at what frequency is it pitched?

_____

**2** Ultrasound can be used to detect flaws in metal, as shown opposite.

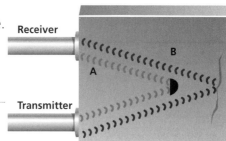

**a)** Which wave, A or B, would arrive back at the receiver first?

_____

**b)** Explain how this arrangement is used to detect flaws.

_____

_____

_____

**3** Explain how ultrasound can be used for cleaning a watch placed in a liquid.

_____

_____

_____

**4** Pregnant women have ultrasound scans to check on the progress of their unborn baby.

**a)** The image produced by ultrasound is not as clear as an image produced by X-rays. Why is ultrasound used for this type of scan instead of X-rays?

_____

**b)** Why is it important to have a very narrow beam of ultrasound waves?

_____

**c)** Describe how ultrasound is used to produce an image of the developing baby.

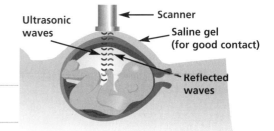

_____

_____

_____

# How Science Works

To answer the questions on this page, you will have to recall scientific facts and draw upon your knowledge of how science works, e.g. scientific procedures, issues and ideas.

**1** Some fishermen are using a boat with an ultrasound detector to help them locate shoals of fish. The fishermen know how long it takes for the ultrasound echo to be reflected off the sea bed at the particular depth that they are fishing at. This can be seen in the diagram opposite. They also know that the speed of sound in water is 1500m/s.

a) Below are three oscilloscope traces produced from the boat's ultrasonic detector. Compare and contrast the oscilloscope traces, and explain what each one means.

i)

ii)

iii)

**b)** If the echo in diagram **iii)** is received after 6000 micro seconds, at what depth should the nets be trawled?

## The Principles of the Motor Effect

**1** What is used to create movement in the motor effect?

**2** Explain what is meant by a magnetic field.

**3** How can the size of a force be increased? Describe two ways.

**a)**

**b)**

**4** How can the direction of a force be reversed? Describe two ways.

**a)**

**b)**

**5** In what circumstances will a conductor carrying an electric current not experience a force?

**6** A direct current motor uses the motor effect (see opposite). When a current flows through the coil, side B moves down.

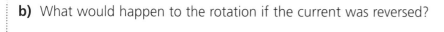

**a)** Why does side A move up?

**b)** What would happen to the rotation if the current was reversed?

# How Science Works

**To answer the questions on this page, you will have to recall scientific facts and draw upon your knowledge of how science works, e.g. scientific procedures, issues and ideas.**

**1** Look at the devices below. Tick two that use the motor effect.

**a)**

☐

**b)**

☐

**c)**

☐

**d)**

☐

**e)**

☐

**f)**

Electric window

☐

**2** Pick one of the devices above that you have ticked and explain, in as much detail as possible, how the motor effect is used.

..............................................................................................................................................................

..............................................................................................................................................................

..............................................................................................................................................................

..............................................................................................................................................................

..............................................................................................................................................................

..............................................................................................................................................................

..............................................................................................................................................................

..............................................................................................................................................................

# Electromagnetic Induction

**1** What produces current in electromagnetic induction?

.......................................................................................................................................................

**2 a)** The diagrams below show a magnet and a coil of wire. The ammeter measures current.
For each diagram show the reading on the ammeter by drawing in the position of the needle.

i)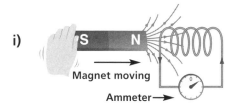

ii)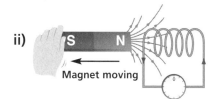

iii)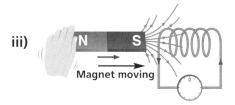

iv)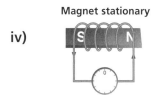

v)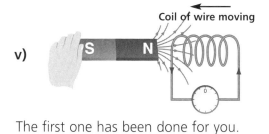

vi)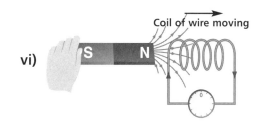

The first one has been done for you.

**b)** Explain why you get a reading on the ammeter.

.......................................................................................................................................................

.......................................................................................................................................................

.......................................................................................................................................................

**3** List three ways of increasing the potential difference created by electromagnetic induction.

**a)** ...........................................................................................................................................

**b)** ...........................................................................................................................................

**c)** ...........................................................................................................................................

# How Science Works

To answer the questions on this page, you will have to recall scientific facts and draw upon your knowledge of how science works, e.g. scientific procedures, issues and ideas.

**1** *An electric generator uses the motor effect to generate electricity.* Is this statement **true** or **false**?

**2** Explain, in your own words, how an alternating current generator works.

**3 a)** On the diagram below, mark the position of the following:

**Rotating coil       Slip rings       Brushes       Generated electricity       Magnetic field**

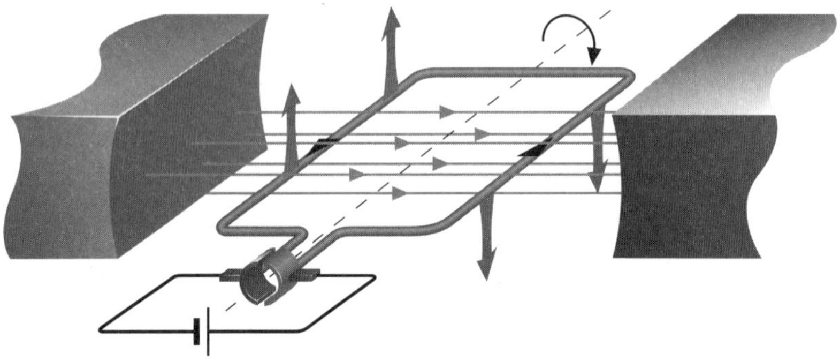

**b)** Explain what the slip rings do.

**c)** Explain what the brushes do.

## Transformers

**1** Explain the difference between a step up and a step down transformer. What are they used for?

........................................................................................................................................................

........................................................................................................................................................

........................................................................................................................................................

**2** Complete the table below for step up and step down transformers.

| Voltage across Primary | Voltage across Secondary | Number of Turns on Primary | Number of Turns on Secondary | Step up or step down? |
|---|---|---|---|---|
| 12V | 240V | 100 | | |
| 400 000V | 200V | | 1 000 | |
| 25 000 | | 20 000 | 20 | |
| | 230V | 150 | 1 500 | |

**3** By what equation is the potential difference across the primary and secondary coils of a transformer related?

........................................................................................................................................................

........................................................................................................................................................

**4** *In a step up transformer the potential difference across the secondary coil is less than the potential difference across the primary coil.* Is this statement **true** or **false**?

........................................................................................................................................................

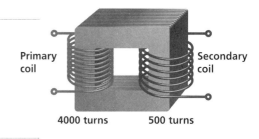

Primary coil          Secondary coil

4000 turns          500 turns

**5** The diagram opposite shows a transformer.

**a)** Name the material used to make the core of the transformer.

........................................................................................................................................................

**b)** Is this a step up or step down transformer? ........................................................................................

**c)** If the primary voltage is 1840V, what is the output voltage?

........................................................................................................................................................

**d)** Explain, in as much detail as you can, how the transformer works.

........................................................................................................................................................

........................................................................................................................................................

........................................................................................................................................................

........................................................................................................................................................

# How Science Works

To answer the questions on this page, you will have to recall scientific facts and draw upon your knowledge of how science works, e.g. scientific procedures, issues and ideas.

**1** What kind of transformer would be used in each of the following situations? Explain your answers.

**a)** Generator ⟶ Power lines

_____

_____

**b)** Mains ⟶ 13V Hairdryer

_____

_____

**c)** Power lines ⟶ Mains

_____

_____

**d)** Mains ⟶ 250V Power drill

_____

_____

**e)** Mains ⟶ 220V Coffee maker

_____

_____

**2 a)** What is the voltage of mains electricity in the UK?

_____

**b)** The mains electricity in America is 110/120V. To use a UK electrical device in America what kind of transformer would you need?

_____

**c)** To use an American electrical device in the UK what kind of transformer would you need?

_____

## Formation of Stars

**1** Describe, in as much detail as possible, how stars like our Sun are formed.

**2** How were the planets formed in our Solar System?

## Our Galaxy and the Universe

**3** What is a galaxy?

**4** Describe how distances between stars in galaxies compare to distances between galaxies within the Universe.

**5** Rewrite the following in order of relative size, starting with the smallest:

**Universe, Planet, Galaxy, Solar System, Star**

**6** Sketch a diagram showing where our Sun fits into the Universe as a whole.

## The Life Cycle of a Star

**1** Our Sun is currently going through a stable period in its life cycle. Describe the forces at work during this stable period.

.......................................................................................................................................................................

.......................................................................................................................................................................

**2** The two flow diagrams below show the cycle of change which occurs when a star dies. Each circle shows what is formed at the end of each change. Complete each circle in the cycle by using the following words: **Supernova, Red giant, Neutron star, Red super giant, White dwarf**

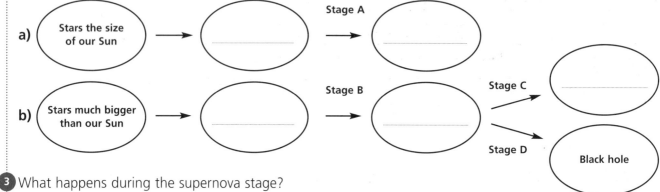

**3** What happens during the supernova stage?

.......................................................................................................................................................................

.......................................................................................................................................................................

**4** We cannot see a black hole directly. Explain why, and therefore how, we can tell where a black hole is.

.......................................................................................................................................................................

.......................................................................................................................................................................

## Recycling Stellar Material

**5** **a)** If all stars were originally formed from hydrogen, explain why there are now many different elements in the Universe, not just hydrogen.

.......................................................................................................................................................................

.......................................................................................................................................................................

.......................................................................................................................................................................

**b)** What evidence do we have of this?

.......................................................................................................................................................................